THE SOUTHERN WHITE RHINOCEROS

The Fierce and Fabulous African Beast

Walt S. Smith, M.S.

Amazon-KDP Publishing

This book is dedicated to my late cousin, Matthew Scott Davis. We were both born on the exact same date and shared a very close bond for many years. Rest-in-Peace, my brother

CONTENTS

Title Page

Copyright

Dedication

Preface

Introduction

Chapter One-Subspecies   1

Chapter Two-Conservation   6

Chapter Three-Reproduction   10

Chapter Four-Communication   16

Chapter Five-Survival Threats   20

Chapter Six-Relationships with other Animals   23

Chapter Seven-White Rhino Facts   26

Epilogue   29

Acknowledgement   31

About The Author   33

Works Cited   35

PREFACE

At Zoo Atlanta, we all patiently waited to see if the two Southern White Rhinos would successfully mate. Well, they finally did. On Christmas Eve, little Zuri was born to her parents, Mumbles and Kiazi. The name is of Swahili origin and means "beautiful" which is certainly the case when it comes to this super high-energy bundle of fun.

I was never really into Rhinoceroses prior to this wonderful event. I love all animals but rhinos were just not on my radar as much as some of the other animals like the giraffes and hornbills, for instance. I will admit that all of the buzz and excitement pulled me in and the birth of not-so-little Zuri had me hooked for life on these amazing creatures.

So I started reading, researching, and observing the rhinos (at each and every volunteer shift that I did) and I began to truly appreciate the very complex animals that they are. I now share everything that I learned on-the-job and during my personal research with my readers. Learn all about the Southern White Rhinoceros within the pages of this book and then follow Randy the Rhino through an amazing adventure in his native land and across the rugged Savannah in the children's book that is a part of this special series.

Walt S. Smith

INTRODUCTION

The Southern White Rhinoceros (*Ceratotherium simum simum*) is an astounding physical specimen. Considering the extraordinary size of this animal, its agility is simply incredible. This particular species of rhino is actually the largest living land animal behind that of the elephant. They have short necks and their heads are normally carried very low to the ground. The male rhinos are slightly heavier than the female rhinos. They have two medial horns that are located on the snout. The front horn is quite a bit longer than the other horn. The name white rhino is derived from the African word "wyt" meaning wide, referring to the broad, square, upper-lipped mouth that distinguishes it from the black rhino. Zoo patrons love to ask why the rhino is not the color, white, so now we have the perfect explanation.

One fascinating fact is that the white rhino has no front teeth. Also, the ears are long and they move around freely. The white rhinos coloration is a slate gray or sometimes even a yellowish-brown. It is definitely not white as the name suggests. They have very little hair except for around their ears, some on the eyelashes, and a few tail bristles rounds it out.

The primary habitat for the white rhino is within vast, open, grassy fields and bushy woodland-type areas that are part of the savannah. Rhinoceroses are also interesting in that they can go without water for four to five days or so and this special survival skill comes in handy when conditions are especially dry on the vast savannah. Read on to discover much more about these rhinoceroses.

CHAPTER ONE- SUBSPECIES

There are two different subspecies of the white rhinoceros: the southern and the northern. Most of the southern species, *Ceratotherium simum simum*, is located in South Africa. The northern species, *Ceratotherium simum cottoni*, have not been seen in quite a while but there were a few of them spotted within the Garamba National Park located in the Congo. The numbers of the northern white variety have declined drastically over many years. In the past few years only a total of four have been spotted. They have not been seen recently and this subspecies may have become extinct in the wild which is sad (see Figure 1). As far as distinguishing between the two different subspecies, the Northern variety are normally: smaller in size, lighter in weight, and have less hair than the Southern subspecies.

Figure 1
Northern White Rhino Chart
Toronto Zoo | Animals

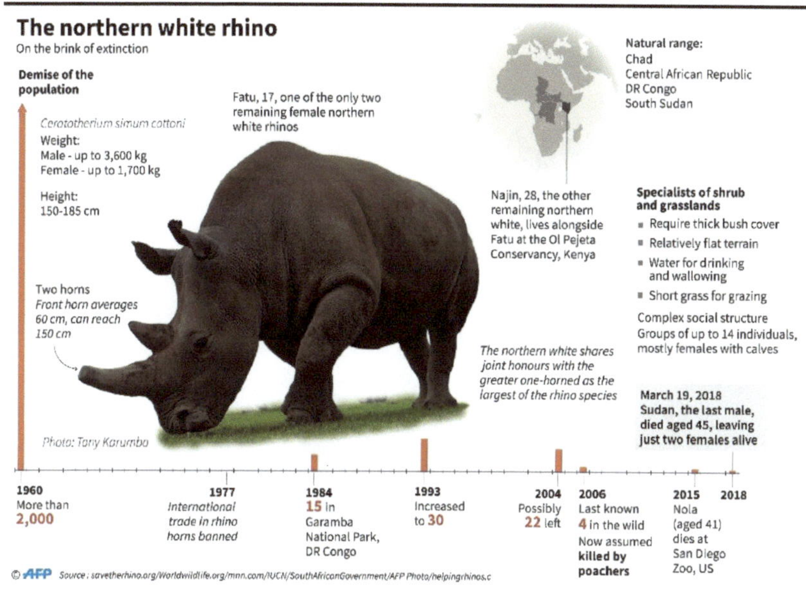

In contrast, the southern species has made a tremendous comeback as the numbers have risen steadily since the late 1960s (see Figure 2).

Figure 2
Southern White Rhinoceros Graphic
Toronto Zoo | Animals

White rhino
(near threatened)

In the wild 19,682-21,077
In AZA[1] zoos 180

Other rhino species

Black 5,042-5,455
(critically endangered)

Greater one-horned 3,500[2]
(vulnerable)

Sumatran 80[2]
(critically endangered)

Javan 67
(critically endangered)

LOSS RISK:

LOWER   THREATENED   EXTINCT

1 — Association of Zoos and Aquariums; 2 — Or fewer

Northern white rhinos are nearly extinct, with only two females remaining in the Democratic Republic of Congo

Figure 3
Closeup of a White Rhino on a South African Safari
Download date: Aug 20, 2024. Licensor author: wirestock - Freepik.com Licensee: user159700887.

"It is not the strongest of the species that survive, nor the most intelligent, but the one most responsive to change."

--- Charles Darwin

CHAPTER TWO- CONSERVATION

Back in the twentieth century, white rhinoceroses were at the very edge of extinction. However, following years of deliberate protection and many relocations of the few hundred or so existing white rhinos back then, this subspecies made a substantial comeback. There are now respectable sized populations that are found within several national parks, reserves, and so on. There are also smaller, reintroduced populations within its former range in Botswana, Namibia, Swaziland, and even Zimbabwe. They have been introduced outside of their former range to Kenya, Uganda, and also Zambia.

Figure 4
Southern White Rhino Chart
Toronto Zoo | Animals

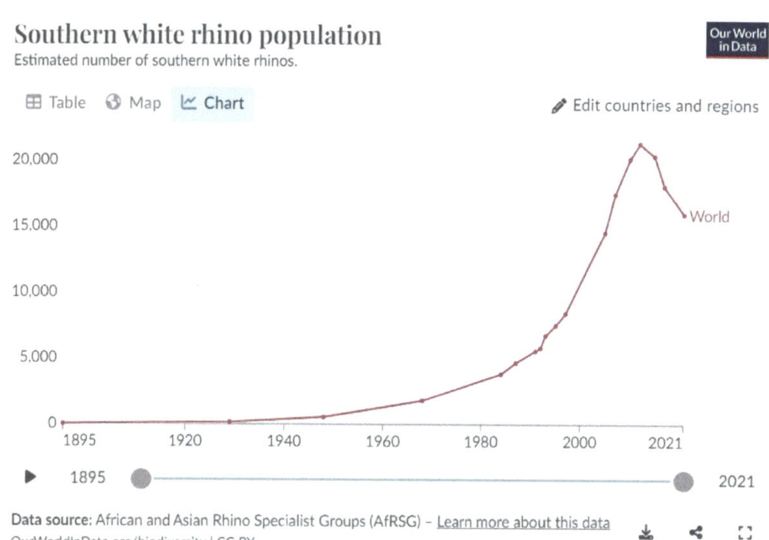

Figure 5
Closeup of a white rhino on a South African safari. Download date: Aug 20, 2024. Licensor™ author: wirestock Freepik.com Licensee: user 159700887.

CHAPTER THREE- REPRODUCTION

The white rhinoceros has a complex social structure as the female rhinos associate with the young rhinos within groups in contrast to the males which are basically solitary and are also extremely territorial. The rhino bulls carefully mark and defend their territories against approaching, unwelcome males. The males allow female rhinos to wander in and through their territories in search of new food sources.

Breeding occurs throughout the year. Before mating, bulls often fight over the females. A form of courtship then takes place and the rhino pair often chase each other and clash horns. The male gives out a call when approaching a female. If she acts aggressively he will stay away. Breeding pairs stay together for only about five to twenty days before they go their separate ways.

A single calf is born after a gestation period of about 16 months. Newborn calves stand up in only a few hours following birth. They nurse at any opportunity, and though they begin eating solid greens when they are only one week old, they will continue to nurse for over a year. A particularly interesting fact is that the calves generally lead their mothers and determine the direction of travel. The mothers are very protective of their calves and will fight vigorously to defend their safety. During any such confrontations the calf will stand behind or to the side of its mother until danger has passed. Young rhinos stay with their mothers for two to three years, leaving only when the mother chases them off before giving birth to the next calf. Considering the prolonged gestation period and only carrying a single young at a time, there is a lot at stake for each calf but after the mothers have done everything they can to prepare the youngster, off into the World it must go. White rhinos live for approximately 40-50 years.

Figure 6
White Rhino Female and Offspring. Download date: Aug 20, 2024.
Licensor™ author: wirestock - Freepik.com Licensee: user159700887.

Figure 7
White Rhino Female and Offspring. Download date: Aug 20, 2024.
Licensor™ author: wirestock - Freepik.com Licensee: user159700887.

"The greatest threat to our planet is the belief that someone else will save it."

--- Robert Swan

CHAPTER FOUR- COMMUNICATION

The white rhinos have about ten different vocalizations, including a panting type of call, along with grunts, some snorting sounds that are associated with the courtship process, distress squeals, and deep growls when they are threatened. The males exhibit various threat displays such as that of wiping its horn on the ground and even a head-low posture with ears back with snarl sounds. The most serious fights break out over mating rights over a female. They create communal dung heaps, which facilitate olfactory identification between animals in an area. Dominant bulls mark their territory with excrement and urine. They also may scatter their dung after defecation. Another way of marking their territory is by wiping horns on bushes or the ground and scrapes with its feet before urine spraying. This ritual (urine marking), except without spraying, is commonly used. The territorial male will scrape-mark every 30 meters or so while patrolling its territorial boundary. Subordinate males do not mark territory. Although vision is relatively poor, senses of hearing and smell are acute. Its ears can move independently to pick up more sounds but it depends most of all on smell. The olfactory passages which are responsible for smell are larger than their entire brain.

Figure 8

Closeup of a white rhino on a South African safari Download date: Aug 20, 2024. Licensor™ author: wirestock - Freepik.com Licensee: user159700887.

CHAPTER FIVE- SURVIVAL THREATS

One of the primary threats to the white rhinoceros population is illegal hunting for the international trade in rhino horns. This has escalated greatly in recent years especially with the northern rhino and no doubt greatly led to their demise in the wild. Civil wars have also contributed to threatening white rhino numbers. Rhino horns have two main uses: traditional use in Chinese medicine, and ornamental use. It is highly prized for making ornamental dagger handles (which are called "jambiyas") in Middle Eastern countries. Horn, hide, and flesh are believed to be powerful aphrodisiacs so all three can be obtained from the white rhinoceros. Adult rhinos have no natural predators other than poachers. They are at the very top of the food chain. If humans would simply stop hunting these magnificent creatures, perhaps by way of additional protections put into place, their numbers would reach very respectable levels and that would mean their existence for many generations to come.

Figure 9
Closeup of a white rhino on a South African safari Download date: Aug 20, 2024. Licensor™ author: wirestock - Freepik.com Licensee: user159700887.

CHAPTER SIX- RELATIONSHIPS WITH OTHER ANIMALS

Rhinos are generally active in the early morning, late afternoon, and evening. During the middle of the day, they wallow or rest in the shade. Like all species of rhinoceros they love wallowing in mud holes to cool down. This is especially important during hot weather for purposes of thermoregulation and for ridding the body of ectoparasites which can easily accumulate on these creatures due to their massive size. Rhinos have developed a special relationship with birds such as the oxpecker, the egret, and the bee-eater. This is referred to as commensalism which means that both organisms in question receive some benefit from the relationship. All of these birds mentioned act as sentinels and feed on a wide variety of parasites on the backs of the rhinos.

Figure 10
White Rhino Female and Offspring. Download date: Aug 20, 2024.
Licensor author: wirestock - Freepik.com Licensee: user159700887.

25

CHAPTER SEVEN- WHITE RHINO FACTS

❖ Lifespan: about 40-50 years

❖ Habitat: found primarily in grassland and Savannah

❖ Diet: mostly bush leaves and some small fruits/berries

❖ Weight: well over 5,000 pounds

❖ Height: approximately 6 feet

❖ Calves: weigh about 100-120 pounds

❖ Speed: despite their size, they can run up to 30 mph

❖ Social: the most social of all of the rhinoceros species

❖ Gestation: about 16 months

❖ Horns: the front horn is larger than the other and averages approximately 35 inches in length.

❖ Predation: no natural predators. Only humans are a threat.

EPILOGUE

The white rhinoceros is yet another beautiful, fascinating creature that deserves a safe environment and one without big game trophy hunters chasing it down simply for sport. Specifically, the rhino horn has been such a powerful motivator for hunters and poachers due to its high market value. It almost makes a person wonder that if the rhinoceros was born without the huge, prominent horn, if that would help this animal become much less of a target. It is reasonable to think so but there are plenty of large animals without horns that are hunted for both sport, prestige, and profit. My dream is to eliminate big-game hunting from our universe. I hope that after reading this book about these incredible animals, you will join me in my quest.

Walt S. Smith

ACKNOWLEDGEMENT

I would like to acknowledge all of my professors that patiently worked with me when I struggled with certain zoological or chemistry concepts. They never gave up on me and saw someting in me that I guess at those times I did not see in myself. Thank you!

ABOUT THE AUTHOR

Walt S. Smith

A recent graduate of GSU in Atlanta, Georgia. Walt holds two advanced degrees (MBA and MS). He specializes in writing books about wildlife and marine species. He has worked at both Georgia Aquarium and Zoo Atlanta and his research covers many varieties of animals. In his downtime, he likes to troup fish, hike, go wakeboarding, and run.

WORKS CITED

Southern White Rhinoceros - Fresno Chaffee Zoo

Fresno Chaffee Zoo
894 West Belmont Avenue, Fresno, California 93728

Toronto Zoo | Animals

2000 Meadowvale Road
Toronto, Ontario
M1B 5K7